What Do Plants Need?

Written by Josephine Selwyn

Vital Vocabulary

Plants need soil.

soil

Plants need sunlight.

sunlight

Plants need air.

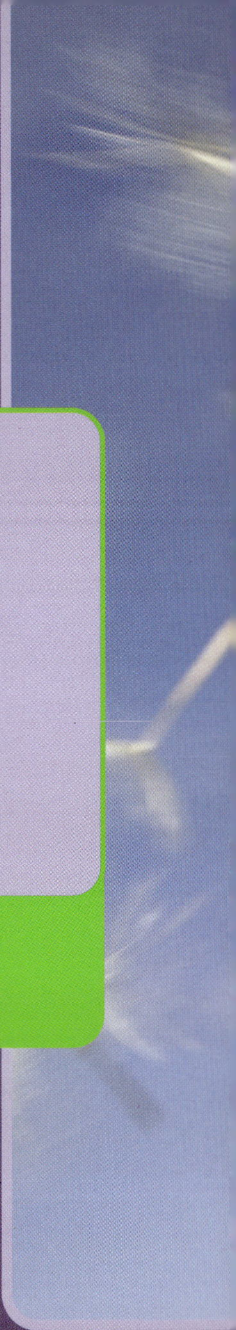

air

Plants need water.

water

Plants need food.

food

Plants need all these things to grow.

water
soil
sunlight
Plants Need
air
food

Critical Thinking

What do you think this plant needs?